FRIENDS OF ACPL

MAR 1
Mar 15
Mar 22 '46
Apr 11 '46
Apr 18 '4
May 23 '46
Nov 14
DEC 5

THE WONDER ROCK
· an indian myth ·

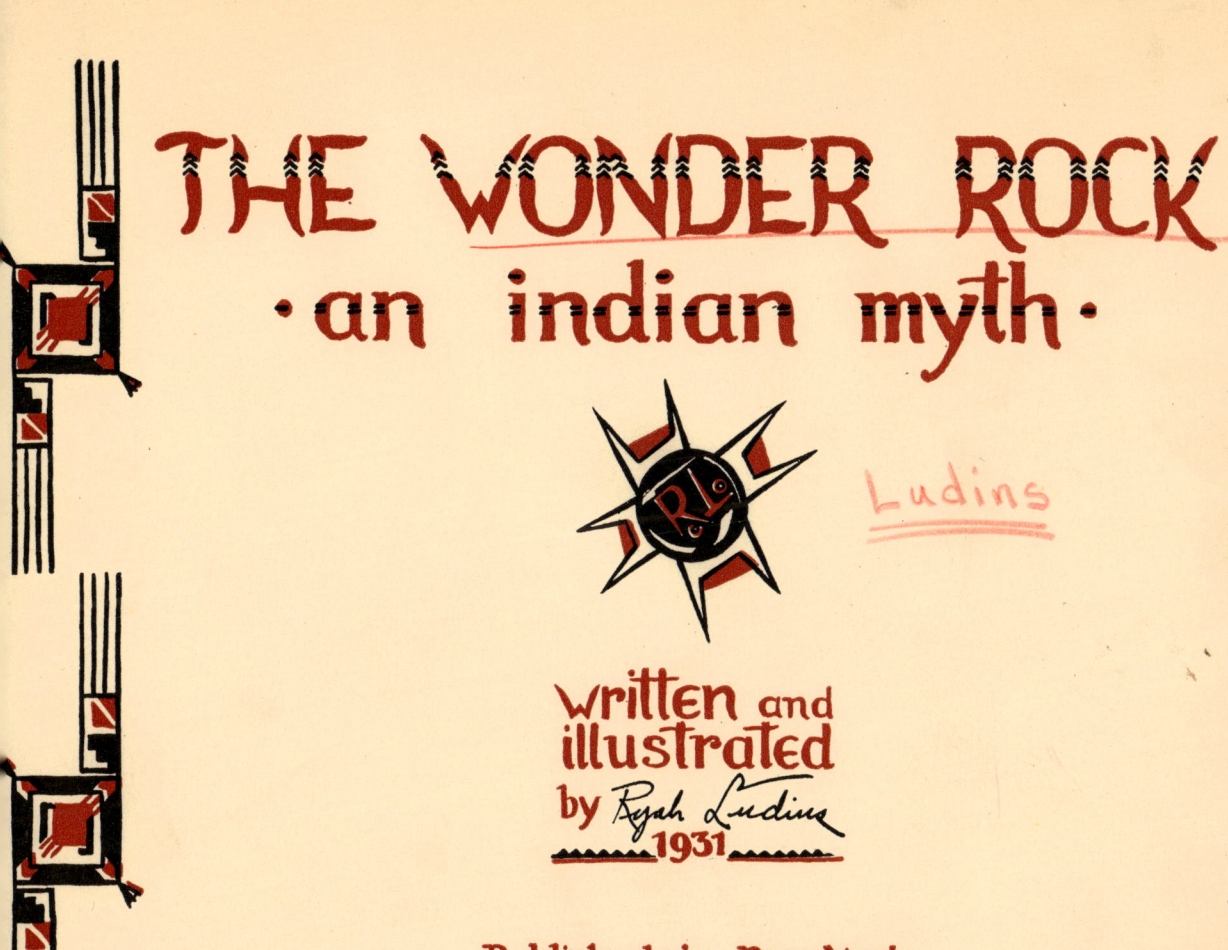

written and illustrated by Ryah Ludins
1931

Published in New York
by COWARD~McCANN, INC.

Copyright 1931 by
• COWARD-McCANN, INC •
All rights reserved

Printed in the
• United States of America •

CO. SCHOOLS

C85295

~introduction~

Here are Wind~Lad and Star~Child,
on a beautiful summer morning
in the Happy Valley..

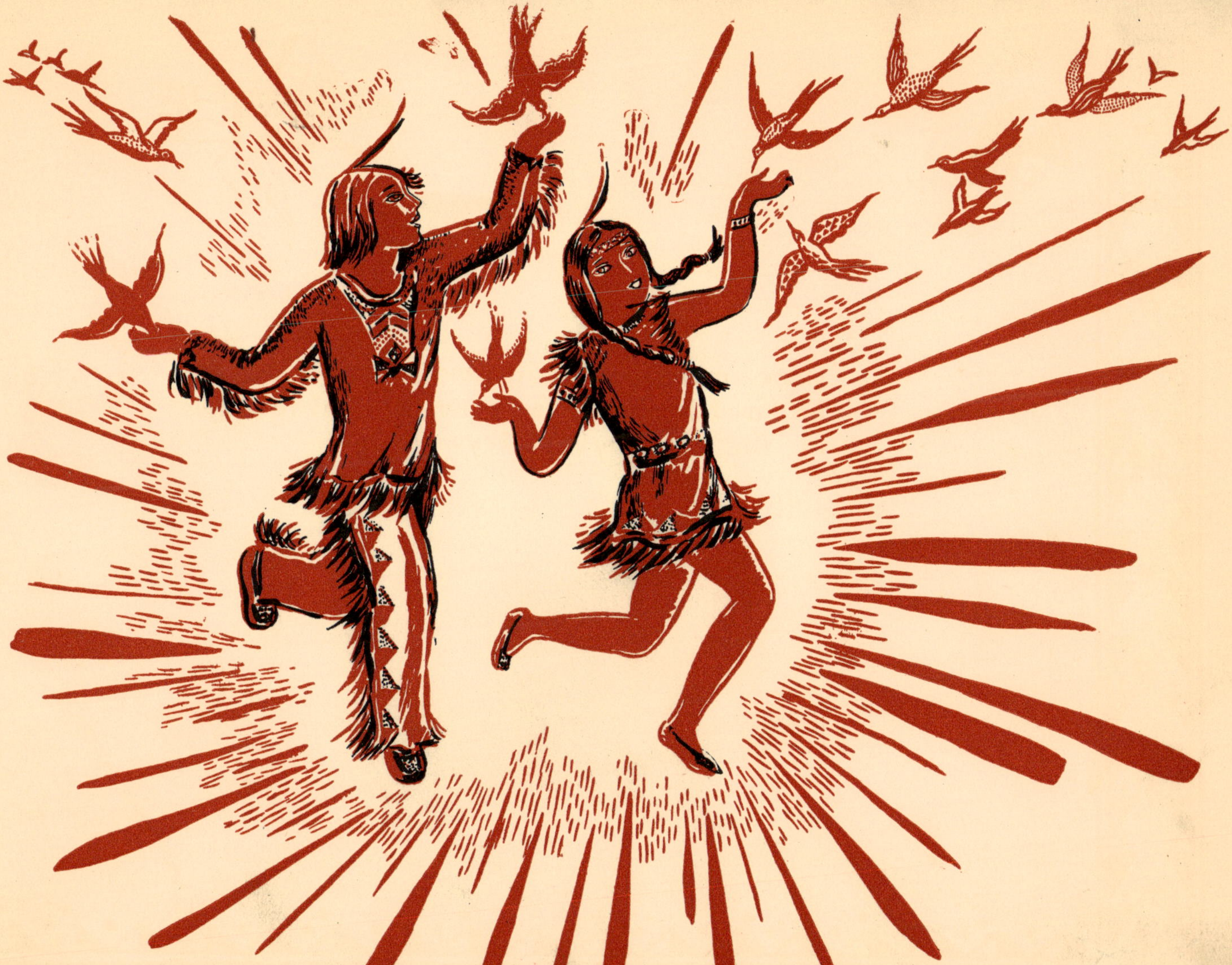

This is The Rock as it looks at the beginning of our story. It becomes more and more important as the story goes on, until it becomes so very important, that if it weren't in the story at the beginning, perhaps there would have been no story at all~~ because then,~~~~ nothing could have really happened~~~ and nothing _would_ have really happened.~~~

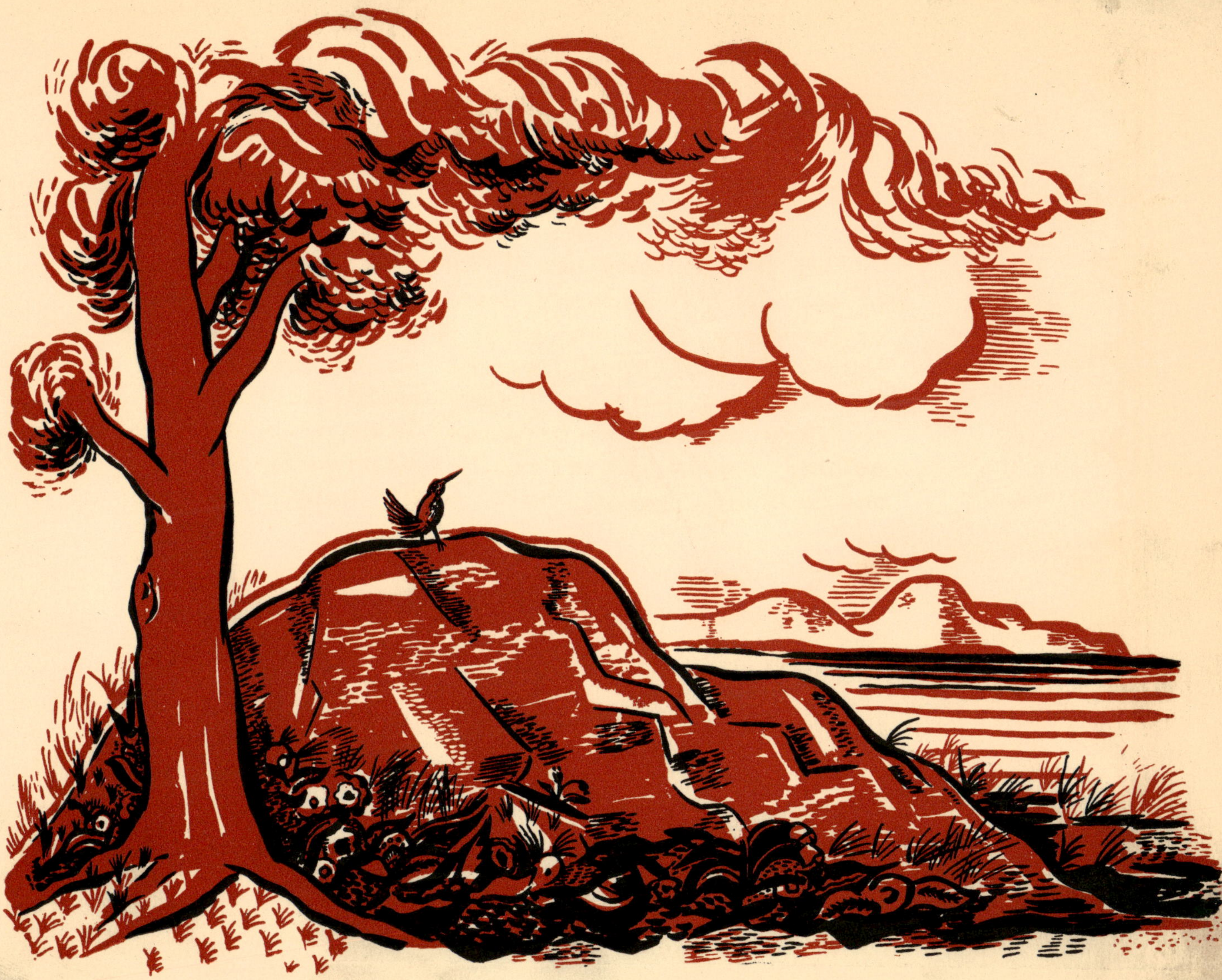

Here are some of the good animals of our story.
~ The small, gentle Mouse.
~ The big, furry, proud Raccoon.
~ The clumsy, heavy and very
    good-natured Grizzly Bear
         ~and~
~ The huge, strong Mountain Lion,
    the king of them all.

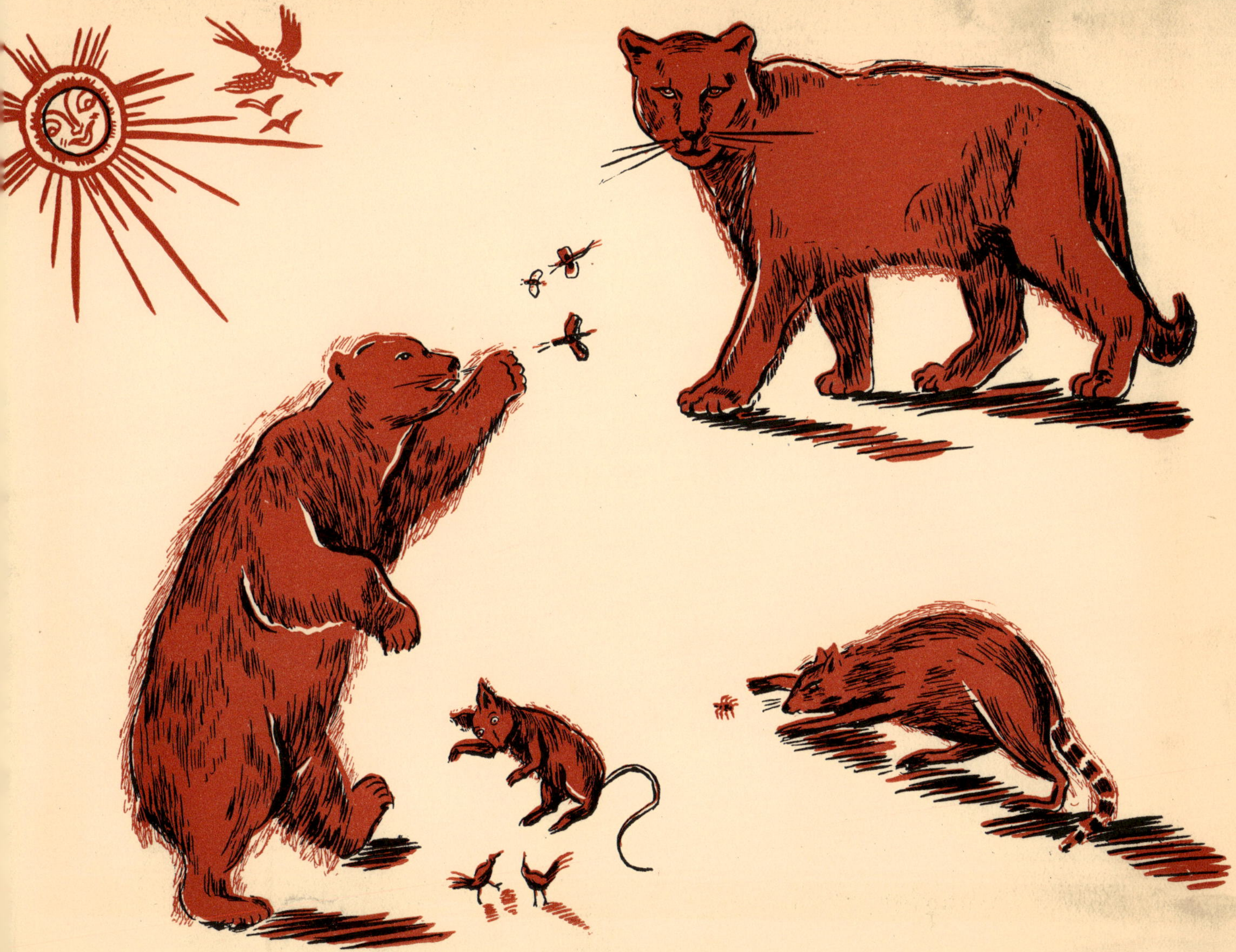

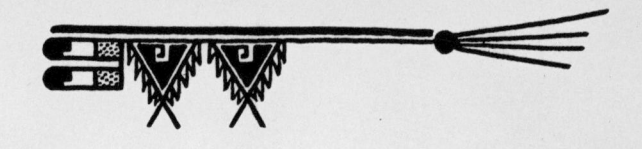

AND~
Last of all~~
    comes.....
        TA~KA~NU~LA, the little, creeping worm. He was all beautifully striped and spotted. His fuzz was fine and silken. But no one ever noticed him or paid the slightest attention to him. No one ever did!!

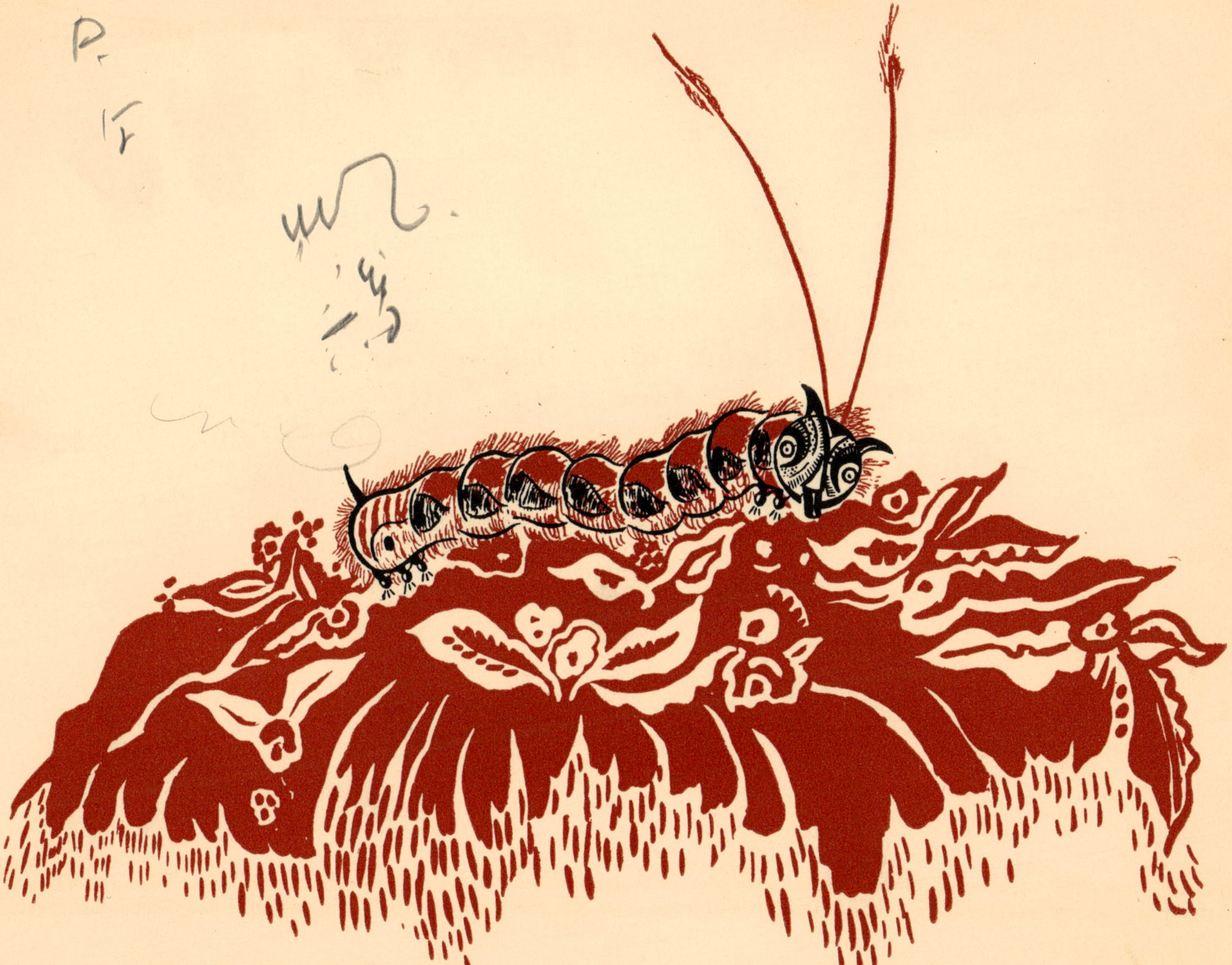

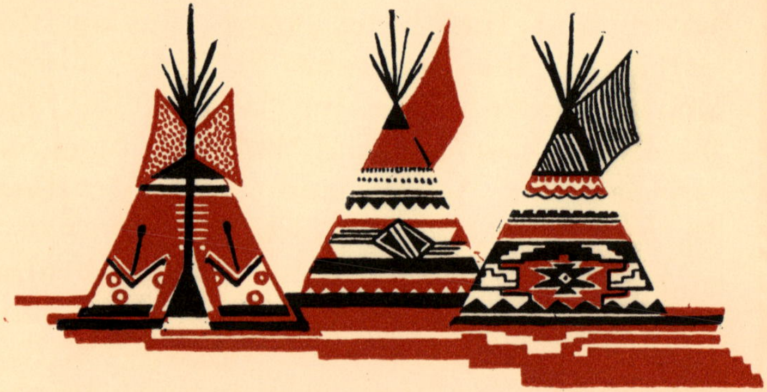

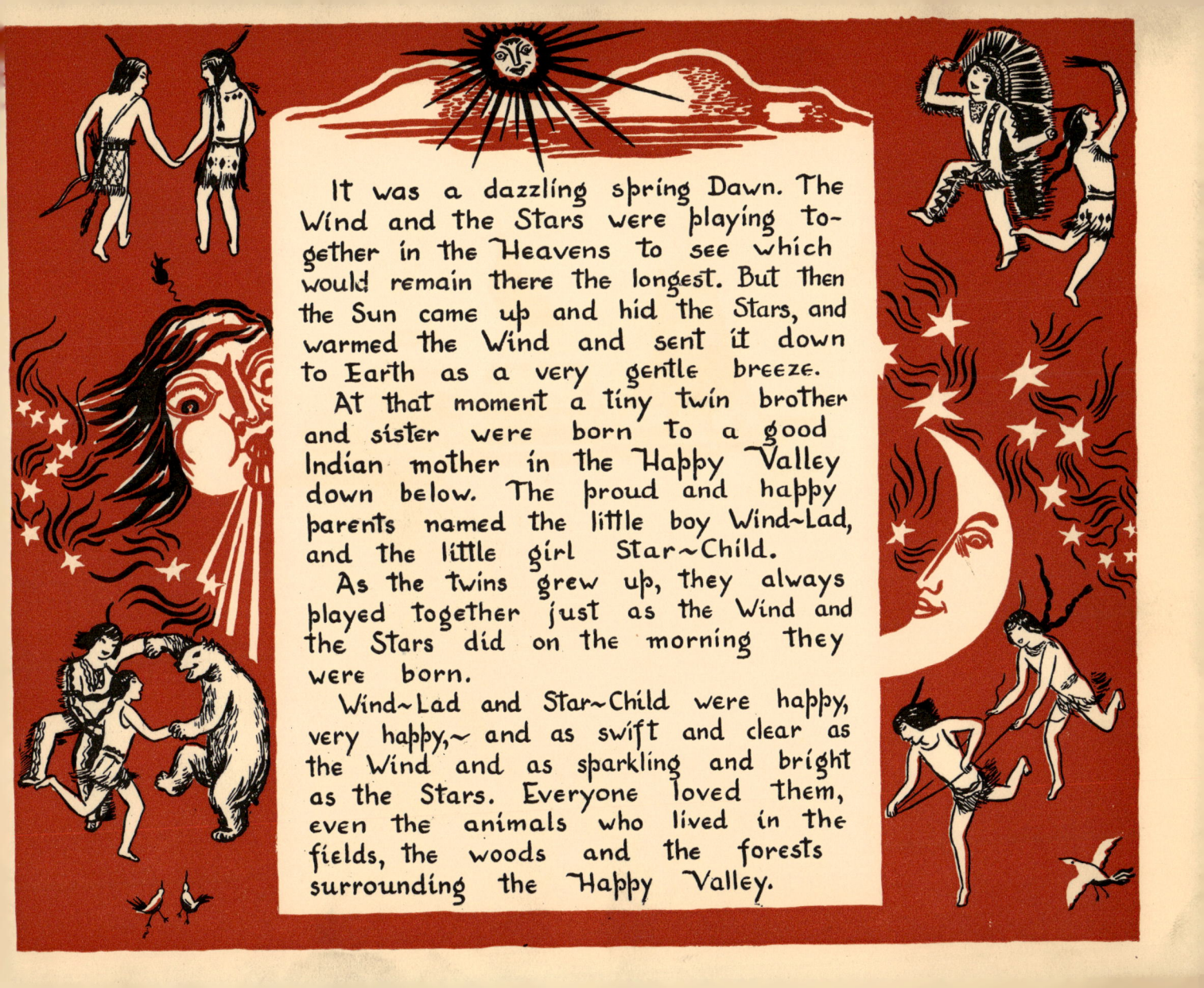

It was a dazzling spring Dawn. The Wind and the Stars were playing together in the Heavens to see which would remain there the longest. But then the Sun came up and hid the Stars, and warmed the Wind and sent it down to Earth as a very gentle breeze.

At that moment a tiny twin brother and sister were born to a good Indian mother in the Happy Valley down below. The proud and happy parents named the little boy Wind~Lad, and the little girl Star~Child.

As the twins grew up, they always played together just as the Wind and the Stars did on the morning they were born.

Wind~Lad and Star~Child were happy, very happy,~ and as swift and clear as the Wind and as sparkling and bright as the Stars. Everyone loved them, even the animals who lived in the fields, the woods and the forests surrounding the Happy Valley.

~Wind~Lad and Star~Child went to the river to swim and to paddle their canoe just as all big Indians do. It was in the summertime. They swam,~ and paddled,~ and splashed around in the water~then~ they splashed and paddled and swam some more, until they became very tired and sleepy.

"Wind~Lad", said Star~Child, "I-I-I, am t-t-ti~rrr~rr~d. I,I, d-d-don't w~w~ant t-t-t- to p-p-pl-lay an~n~ny m~m~o~rrr~e."~~~ Oh! Star~Child did not really stammer or stutter when she spoke. It was just the chattering of her teeth because she had stayed in the cold water too long.~

"Come on, Star-Child," said Wind-Lad, "there is a good spot where we can rest."
They saw an orange-colored Rock sparkling in the Sun. Around it the grass was bright green and soft. One could have found many brilliant flowers growing very happily in it. It all looked so jolly that the two children climbed up on the Rock which was warm from the Sun — and before they knew it — both Wind-Lad and Star-Child fell fast asleep.~~

The Sun shone on Wind~Lad and Star~Child and smiled happily, because it knew that it was warming them. It shone and smiled all day long, until it too became tired~~~
~~~ Then it tucked away its sun~rays and went down behind the blue mountain to sleep~

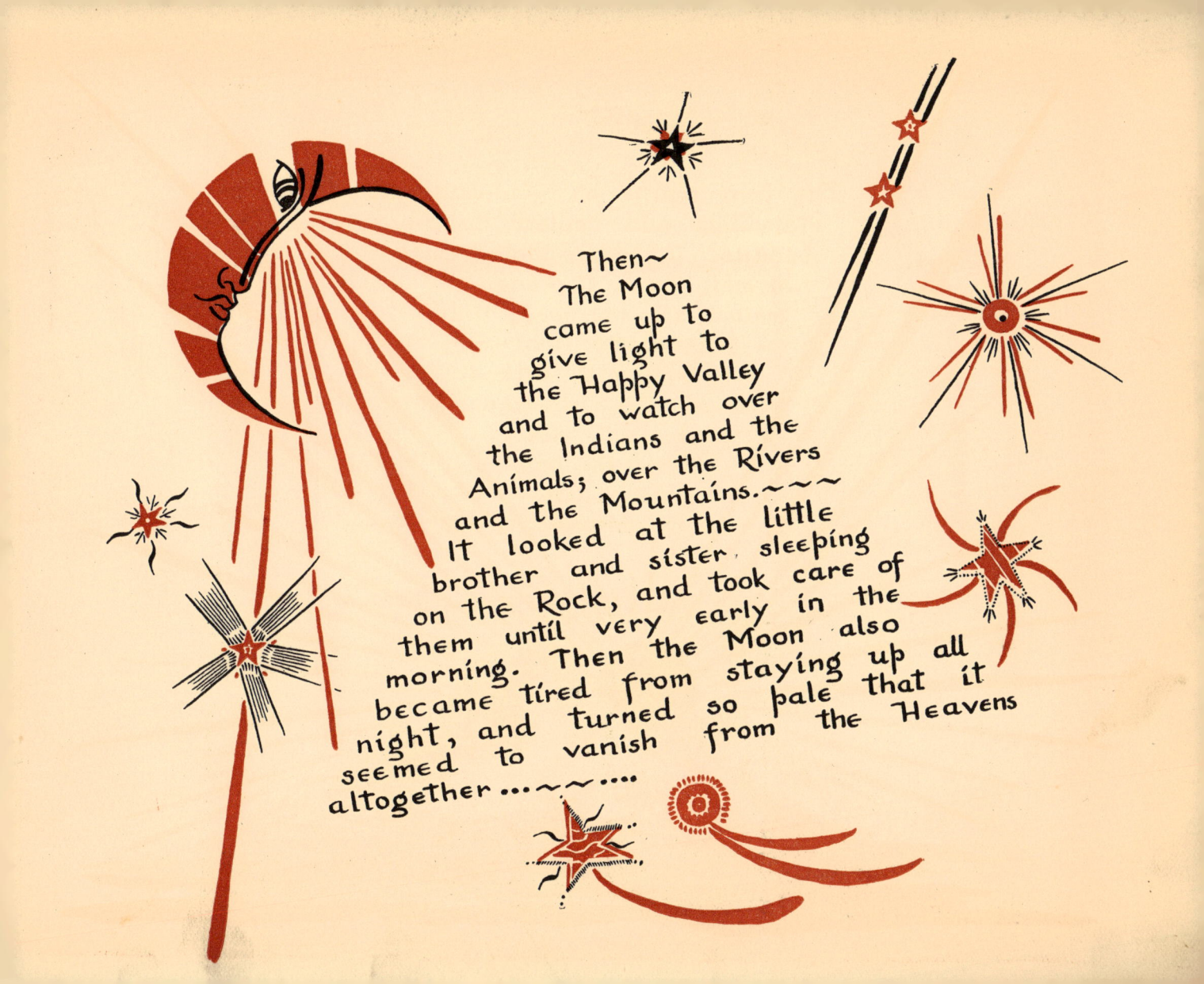

Then~
The Moon came up to give light to the Happy Valley and to watch over the Indians and the Animals; over the Rivers and the Mountains.~~~
It looked at the little brother and sister sleeping on the Rock, and took care of them until very early in the morning. Then the Moon also became tired from staying up all night, and turned so pale that it seemed to vanish from the Heavens altogether...~~....

Days and Nights passed!
The Sun rose and set!
The Moon waxed and waned!
but
Wind-Lad and Star-Child
slept, on~and
on~and~on!

MEANWHILE...

A very strange~and~curious~
and extra-ordinary thing
happened...

~AUTUMN came~~
The Rock on which Wind~Lad and Star~Child fell asleep, began to grow higher and higher~until it was even higher than the tallest oak tree which grew by the side of it.~~
If Wind~Lad and Star~Child had been awake, they could have picked off the brightest orange autumn leaf on the top-most branch.~~~~~~
But~they didn't pick it off, because they slept ON~~ and ON~ and ON~!

~ and then WINTER followed ~
The Rock kept growing higher and higher ~ until Wind-Lad and Star-Child could have played with the snow clouds which began powdering their Happy Valley with the softest, whitest flakes. But they didn't play with the snow clouds, because both Wind-Lad and Star-Child slept ON ~ and ON ~ and ON ~!

~SPRING arrived in all its glory.~ The snow clouds disappeared. The birds flew up and around the high Rock, but they couldn't fly up as high as Wind~Lad and Star~Child and play with them, because the Rock was growing higher and higher up towards the Heavens where no birds could fly. The Rock grew and kept on growing while Wind~Lad and Star~Child slept ON~and ON~and ON~!

~and then SUMMER came again~

The trees were green with leaves; the earth bright with grass and flowers; the rivers and streams filled up with water. But by this time, the Rock was so high that Wind~Lad's and Star~Child's noses almost touched the Sun by day and the Moon by night. Clouds were all over and about them; flaming red clouds, purple and gold clouds,— some with silver linings and some without.~~~~~~

And still the Rock kept growing higher and higher~ while Wind~Lad and Star~Child slept ON~ and ON~ and ON~!

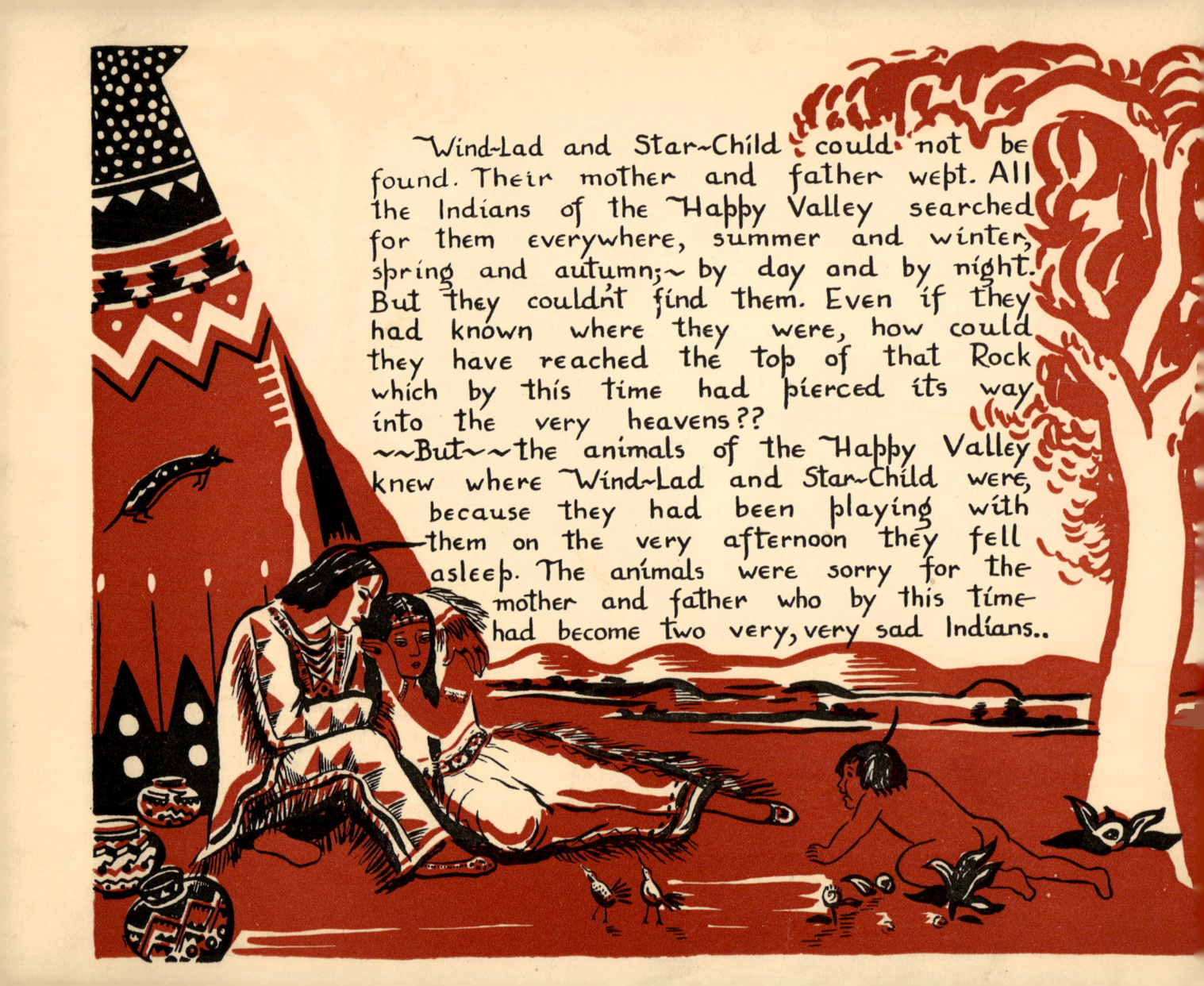

Wind-Lad and Star-Child could not be found. Their mother and father wept. All the Indians of the Happy Valley searched for them everywhere, summer and winter, spring and autumn;~ by day and by night. But they couldn't find them. Even if they had known where they were, how could they have reached the top of that Rock which by this time had pierced its way into the very heavens??
~~But~~ the animals of the Happy Valley knew where Wind-Lad and Star-Child were, because they had been playing with them on the very afternoon they fell asleep. The animals were sorry for the mother and father who by this time had become two very, very sad Indians..

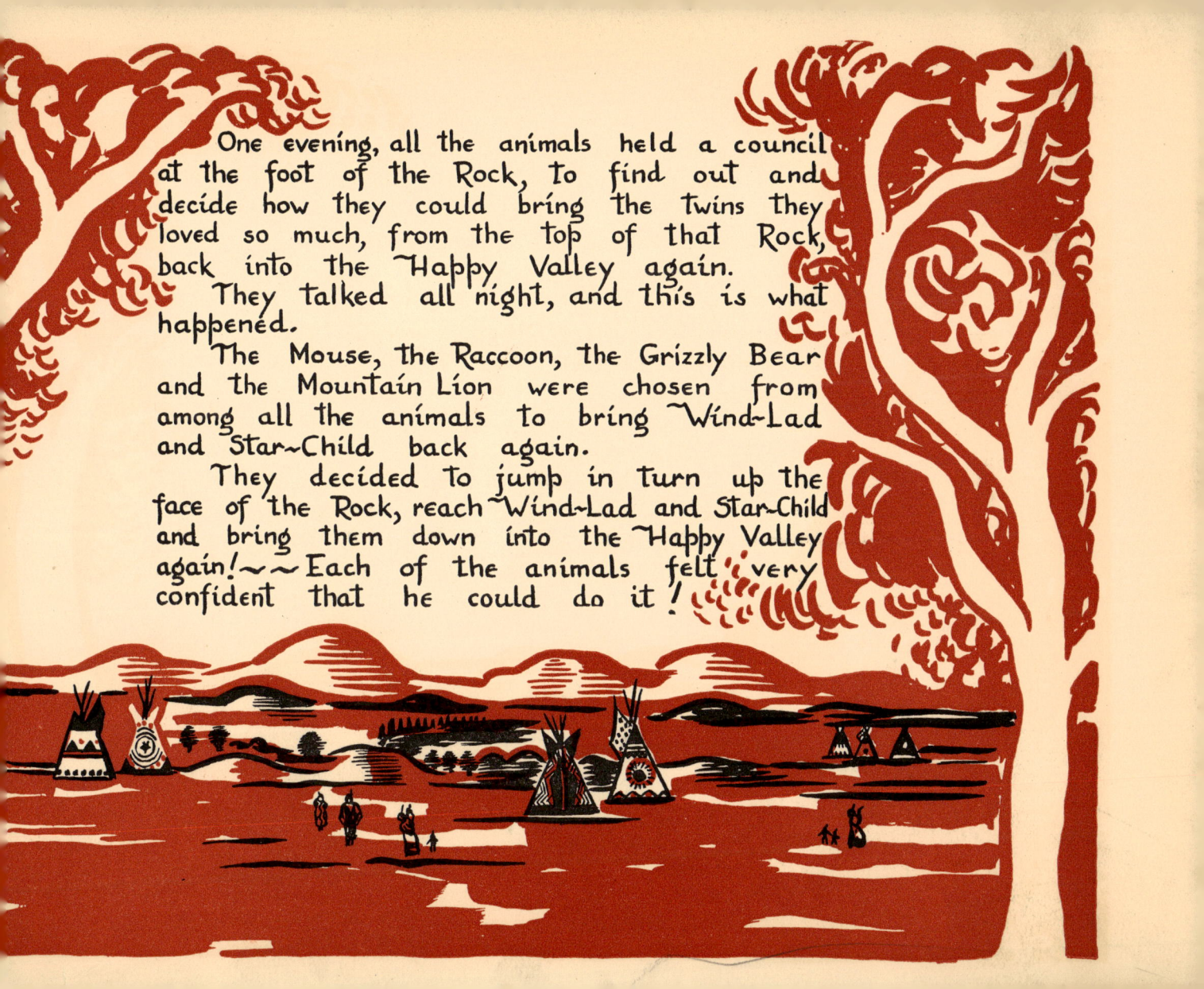

One evening, all the animals held a council at the foot of the Rock, to find out and decide how they could bring the twins they loved so much, from the top of that Rock, back into the Happy Valley again.

They talked all night, and this is what happened.

The Mouse, the Raccoon, the Grizzly Bear and the Mountain Lion were chosen from among all the animals to bring Wind-Lad and Star-Child back again.

They decided to jump in turn up the face of the Rock, reach Wind-Lad and Star-Child and bring them down into the Happy Valley again!~~ Each of the animals felt very confident that he could do it!

~First of all~the Mouse tried.~
    The little gentle Mouse was small, but she was a wonderful jumper.
    ~Well~ she took a great huge jump up the face of the Rock, and went up very, very much higher than any other Mouse could have gone ~ but ~ she didn't reach one-hundredth, not even one-thousandth of the way up. The poor Mouse landed on her back with an awful thump, and scampered away with the speed of a streak of lightning.
    All the other animals thought, "Oh! just wait until I try!"

~The Raccoon~ ~~tried second.~

The fluffy, comfortable looking Raccoon was happy that finally his chance had come to jump. He made a great leap~ and of course went up much, much higher than the little Mouse,~ but~ even that wasn't one-hundredth, not one-thousandth of the way up.

And the poor Raccoon landed on his head, right in the middle of a muddy puddle of water. He felt terribly unhappy and would have kept his head stuck right in the mud from shame, but he couldn't breathe very well. So he wiggled out and sat in the Sun to dry and to watch the Grizzly Bear who was the next to try to jump up the face of the great Rock.

~Third~~~the Grizzly Bear tried.~

The clumsy good-natured Grizzly Bear almost wept. He felt so sorry for both the Mouse and the Raccoon who had such a terrible come-down. Oh! he was sure he would reach the top.

So _he_ tried!!

He jumped and clawed the air with his big paws going up,~ and clawed the air with his big paws coming down and down and down~ and then~ he fell with all the heaviness and clumsiness of a Grizzly Bear. The poor little Mouse hid under a leaf from fright, thinking the great Rock had fallen down.

Even the Grizzly Bear didn't reach one-hundredth, not even one-thousandth of the way up the Rock.

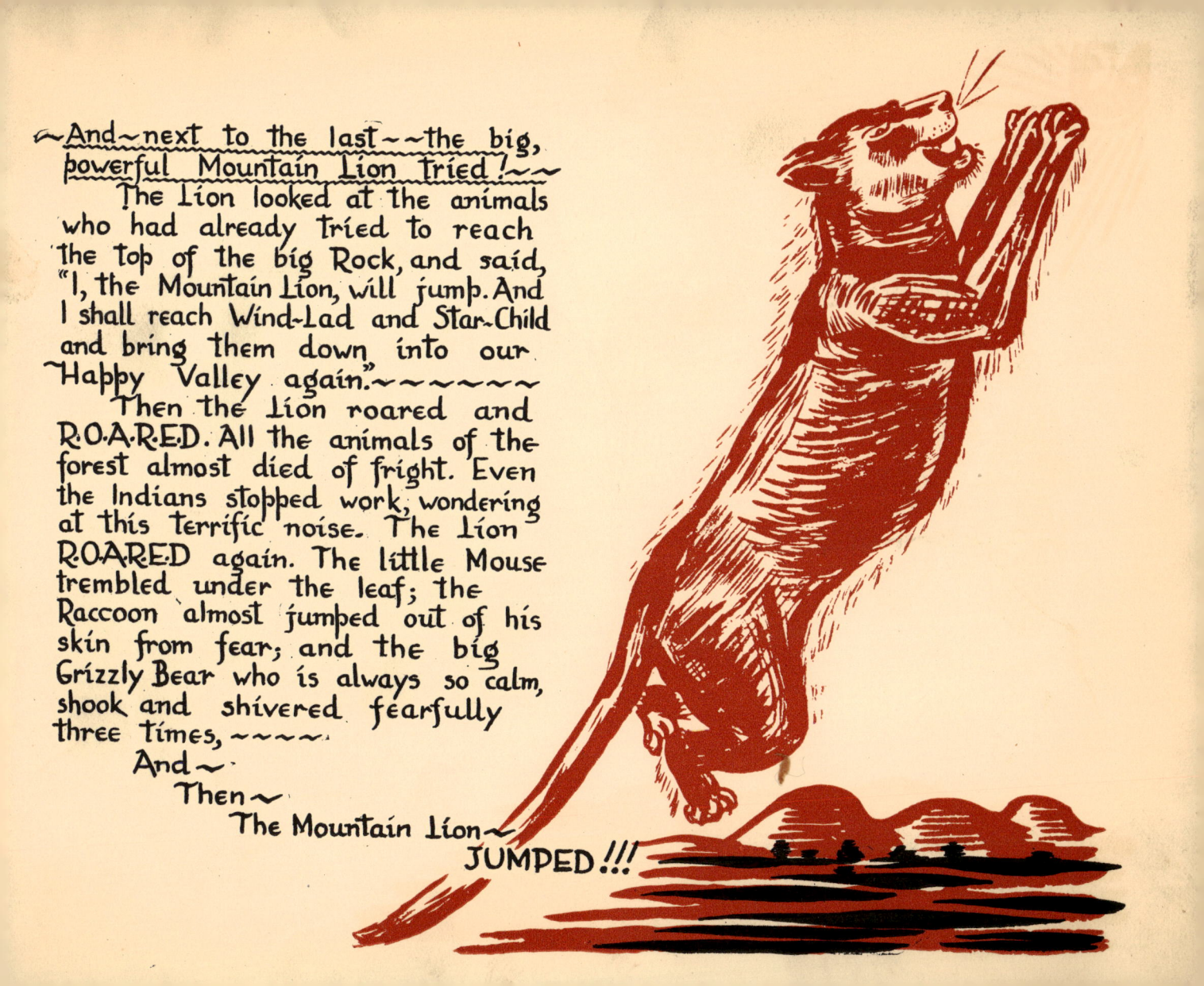

~And~ next to the last~~the big, powerful Mountain Lion tried!~~
   The Lion looked at the animals who had already tried to reach the top of the big Rock, and said, "I, the Mountain Lion, will jump. And I shall reach Wind-Lad and Star-Child and bring them down into our Happy Valley again."~~~~~~
   Then the Lion roared and R.O.A.R.E.D. All the animals of the forest almost died of fright. Even the Indians stopped work, wondering at this terrific noise. The Lion R.O.A.R.E.D again. The little Mouse trembled under the leaf; the Raccoon almost jumped out of his skin from fear; and the big Grizzly Bear who is always so calm, shook and shivered fearfully three times,~~~~
      And~
         Then~
            The Mountain Lion~
               JUMPED !!!

~The Grizzly Bear stood up on his hind legs to see this wondrous sight.~

~The Mouse crawled from under the leaf.~

~The Raccoon crept back, brushing the mud out of his eyes with his paws.

~and~

All the Indians came running towards the Rock. They watched in awe as the Mountain Lion leaped, because he was supposed to be the very last animal to try and bring back Wind-Lad and Star-Child. If the Lion couldn't reach the little twin brother and sister, then no one else could. So thought all the Indians and all the animals of the Happy Valley.~~~

And the Mountain Lion jumped ~high~ very high. But he made exactly nine somersaults in the air, coming down. Even the Lion, the king of them all, couldn't reach one-hundredth of the way up. He did reach one-thousandth of the way up, and he was the only animal to reach at least that far up towards Wind-Lad and Star-Child. But one-thousandth of the way up the face of the Rock was not all the way up.~~

There was mourning in the Happy Valley. The Indians and the animals knew now that they would never see Wind-Lad and Star-Child again. The Indians wailed; the animals cried, each its own peculiar cry; and the poor little mouse squeaked and squeaked with sorrow....

But~during all this time, no one noticed TA~KA~NU~LA, an insignificant worm lying half in the mud and half out, who had watched all the animals jump and fail.

He was very much touched by the wailing Indians, and the crying Animals.

He thought to himself, "I'm only an insignificant worm. I can't jump like the Mouse, the Raccoon or the Bear, or roar like the Lion. I can't even hop or run or move very quickly,~but~I have patience. That's about all I do have. There is no use trying to jump, because even the Lion who jumped the highest of all, could not reach the top of the Rock. What shall I do? What shall I do?"

So~instead of doing anything, TA~KA~NU~LA began to think, which is sometimes a very wise thing to do. And TA~KA~NU~LA thought for a long time. No one knew the worm was thinking, and even if they had known that he was thinking, no one would have paid the slightest attention to him, because, what could a poor worm do or think anyway?

And this is what TA~KA~NU~LA thought out. "I will crawl, crawl, crawl, and crawl up the Rock, even if it takes me a very, very long time. And then, I shall bring Wind~Lad and Star~Child back to the Happy Valley again."

And TA~KA~NU~LA crawled. He crawled through many moons and through many suns; through a whole summer, autumn, winter and spring. He crawled through forests and snow, bramble and water, until he was so high that nothing grew on the Rock any more. It was all just solid, bare rock, without even a blade of grass on it. And TA~KA~NU~LA was hungry. There was nothing to eat. And he was thirsty, but there was nothing to drink. But still he crawled ON and ON and ON. "Oh! I must get to the top. I must! I must! I must!

TA~KA~NU~LA was becoming weaker and weaker. It was two days now since he had eaten the last morsel of food or drunk the last drop of water. His little body was sore and bruised. He crawled slower and slower and often had to rest for a long time. There were many long weary hours when he was sure he could never live to reach the top of the Rock where Wind~Lad and Star~Child were asleep.

And on the third day, a good, kind, warm rain fell from a silver grey cloud right up above him. TA~KA~NU~LA swallowed a few rain-drops and almost immediately began to feel stronger.

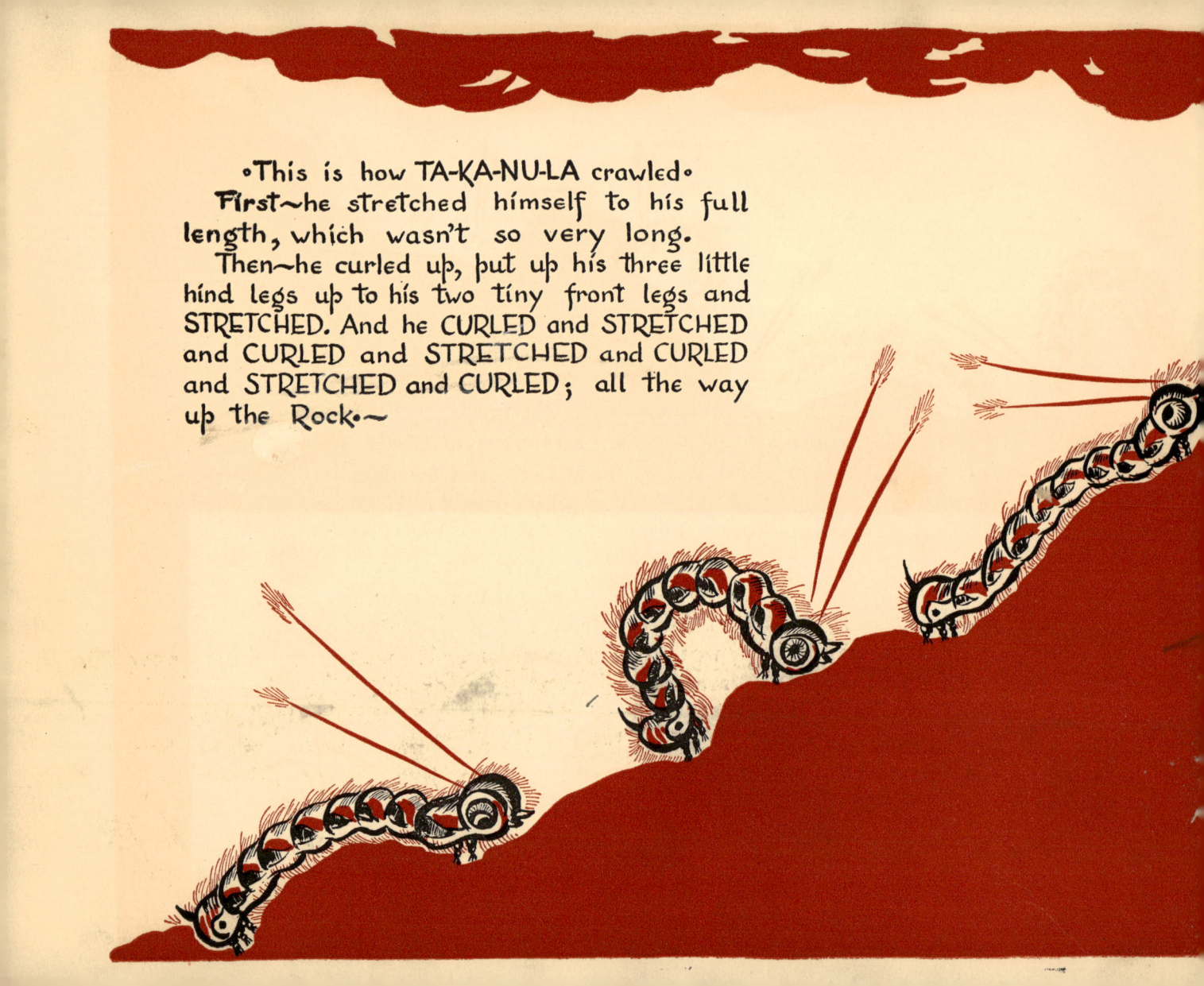

•This is how TA-KA-NU-LA crawled•
First~he stretched himself to his full length, which wasn't so very long.
Then~he curled up, put up his three little hind legs up to his two tiny front legs and STRETCHED. And he CURLED and STRETCHED and CURLED and STRETCHED and CURLED and STRETCHED and CURLED; all the way up the Rock.~

Do this with your hand and fingers if you want to know how TA-KA-NU-LA crawled.

and ~
TA-KA-NU-LA crawled this way with his body, and got there as soon as you would if you had to crawl to the top of the Rock with your fingers.

With a few more crawls TA~KA~NU~LA reached the very toppest top of the Rock.. And what do you think he saw?

On the very highest peak of the Rock, lying on a bed of the softest, greenest moss, Wind~Lad and Star~Child fast asleep!

"How shall I wake them up?", thought TA~KA~NU~LA. He crept all around them, but neither Wind~Lad nor Star~Child stirred. "What shall I do? What shall I do? cried TA~KA~NU~LA. "I climbed to the toppest top of this great Rock, I found Wind~Lad and Star~Child, but I can't wake them up. Oh! what shall I do?" And again, instead of doing anything, TA~KA~NU~LA began to think. A very happy idea struck him. He crept straight up onto Wind~Lad's face and with his little paws began pawing, patting and tickling Wind~Lad's nose and ears and eyes. Wind~Lad blinked one eyelash.. TA~KA~NU~LA felt encouraged..~~~

Then he crawled right over onto Star~Child's face and pawed, rolled and crept all over it until she too began to smile. "Hurrah! hurrah!, they are beginning to stir", said TA~KA~NU~LA.

TA~KA~NU~LA crept over them with his fuzzy, warm body. Wind~Lad and Star~Child began to move, then yawn and blink, and stretch and yawn. Then they smiled, grinned and giggled as TA~KA~NU~LA crept over their eyes and noses, awakening them with his tickly fuzz. And finally they laughed and awoke.

"Where are we?"~~"What is this?", said Wind~Lad and Star~Child together.~ But TA~KA~NU~LA answered, "Don't ask any questions. Your mother and father, and all the Indians and animals of the Happy Valley are waiting for you. We have a long trip ahead of us. Just trust yourselves to me and I shall tell you all about it on our long journey down the great Rock."

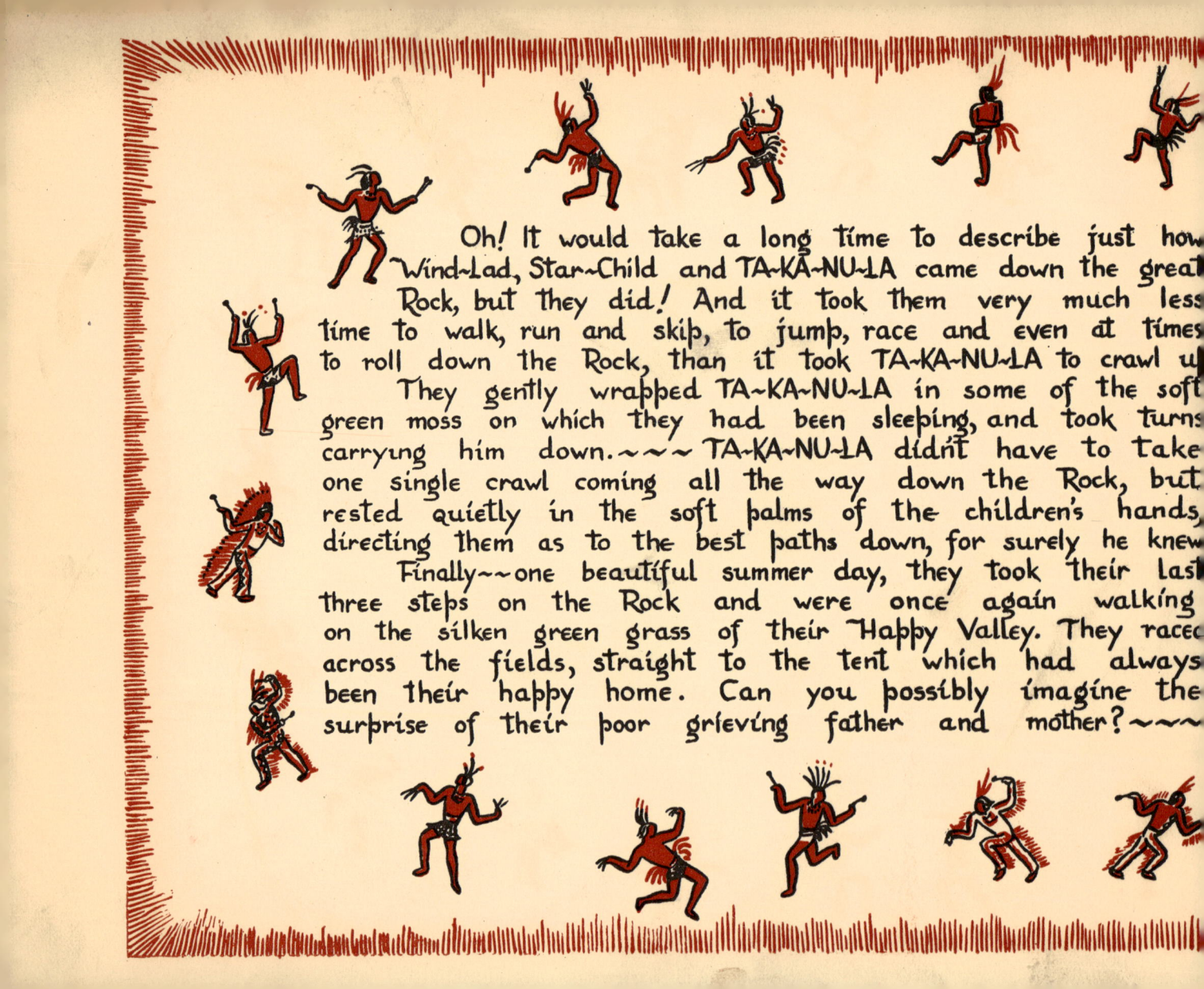

Oh! It would take a long time to describe just how Wind~Lad, Star~Child and TA~KA~NU~LA came down the great Rock, but they did! And it took them very much less time to walk, run and skip, to jump, race and even at times to roll down the Rock, than it took TA~KA~NU~LA to crawl up.

They gently wrapped TA~KA~NU~LA in some of the soft green moss on which they had been sleeping, and took turns carrying him down. ~~~ TA~KA~NU~LA didn't have to take one single crawl coming all the way down the Rock, but rested quietly in the soft palms of the children's hands, directing them as to the best paths down, for surely he knew.

Finally~~one beautiful summer day, they took their last three steps on the Rock and were once again walking on the silken green grass of their Happy Valley. They raced across the fields, straight to the tent which had always been their happy home. Can you possibly imagine the surprise of their poor grieving father and mother? ~~~

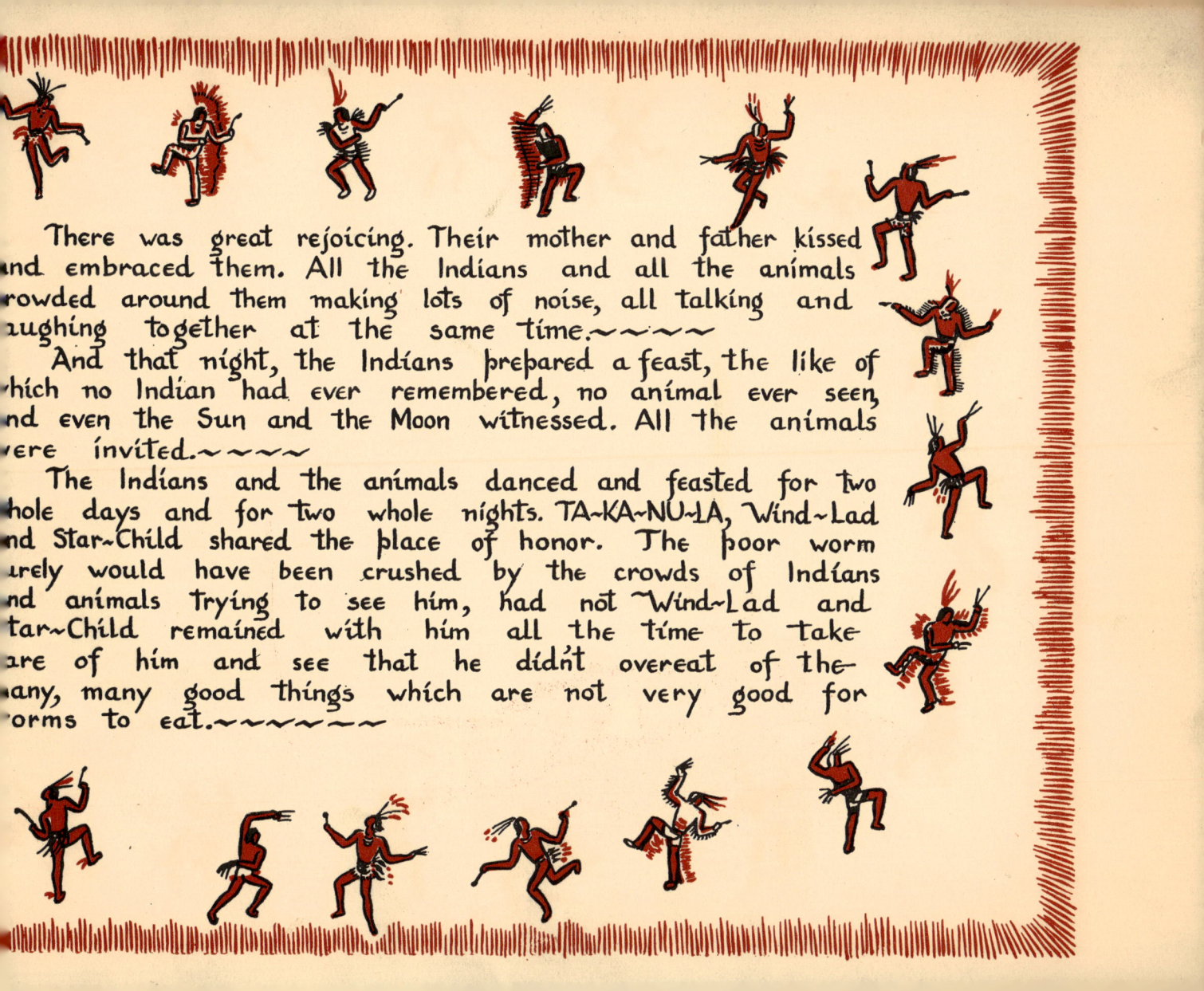

There was great rejoicing. Their mother and father kissed and embraced them. All the Indians and all the animals crowded around them making lots of noise, all talking and laughing together at the same time.~~~~

And that night, the Indians prepared a feast, the like of which no Indian had ever remembered, no animal ever seen, and even the Sun and the Moon witnessed. All the animals were invited.~~~~

The Indians and the animals danced and feasted for two whole days and for two whole nights. TA~KA~NU~LA, Wind~Lad and Star~Child shared the place of honor. The poor worm surely would have been crushed by the crowds of Indians and animals trying to see him, had not Wind~Lad and Star~Child remained with him all the time to take care of him and see that he didn't overeat of the many, many good things which are not very good for worms to eat.~~~~~~

And that evening, the Indians gathered at the command of their chief, around the camp-fire. All the animals also came to listen to his words of wisdom.~~~
  "This is what the chief said.~
"What all our good friends, the animals of the forest, the wood and the field could not do by leaping and jumping;~ what we Indian men did not know how to do; this little worm TA~KA~NU~LA did!! He has never been noticed by anyone, and disliked by everyone when noticed. But now we all love him. TA~KA~NU~LA did this great deed by careful thought, much patience and lots of hard work. Every year on this day, all the Indians of our Happy Valley, and all the animals of the forest, the wood and the field, will meet here at the foot of the great Wonder Rock.~ And then we shall feast and celebrate and honor the big deeds of little TA~KA~NU~LA."~~~~~